GETTING THE BIGGER PICTURE IN YOUR DIVORCE

(And It's Not the 60" T.V.)

A PRACTICAL GUIDE TO DIVORCE AND BLENDED FAMILIES

Paula Kidd Casey

PublishAmerica
Baltimore

First printing

ISBN: 1-60474-977-6
PUBLISHED BY PUBLISHAMERICA, LLLP
www.publishamerica.com
Baltimore

Printed in the United States of America

Nothing in this book should be construed as legal advice, and you should always contact an attorney to answer specific issues regarding your personal situation.

TABLE OF CONTENTS

INTRODUCTION

Divorce. The concept evokes a myriad of emotions and reactions. To some, it conjures up fear, apprehension and uncertainty. To others, it represents relief and a new beginning. Still others are haunted by guilt and remorse.

Divorce is a reality in today's society. It has touched virtually everyone's life...perhaps even yours. Some statistics place divorce rates at over a staggering 60%. The way a divorce is handled both during and after the legal proceedings will affect many lives, now and into the future. To minimize the negative effect this reality may have, it is necessary to obtain as much information as possible to make informed decisions and positive plans for the future. I hope this small book will offer some ideas and options perhaps not heretofore considered.

I am a divorce attorney. Yes, I know that's exactly who Shakespeare had in mind when he said, "Kill all the lawyers." I am also aware that's tantamount to admitting I have horns and a pitchfork. However, it has given me a view of this arena that may be helpful during this stressful period. I have practiced law for over 28 years. I have seen good ways to handle divorce as well as those that are reprehensible. I have seen divorces that were absolutely necessary and healthy, as well as many that were unnecessary and hasty. There were many divorces in between the two ends of the spectrum. However, necessary or not, I have found the parties involved are usually ill prepared, let alone ready, to appropriately handle the necessary steps required in a divorce. Also, they are almost never prepared to navigate the rest of their lives after the proceedings. While marriage may not be forever, divorce is!

If what I have learned from the years of exposure to the heartbreak and upheaval of divorce can help just one person avoid some pitfalls and mistakes, then these suggestions are worth considering. I have been on the front lines of the divorce wars. As the hired gun, I have seen the causalities. I have seen the resulting hurt and injuries when the participants fail to keep the *big picture* in mind. I have also seen the positive outcomes arising from the enlightened few who saw the *big picture* and took it. And I am here to advocate for the *big picture*, the road less taken, the higher ground, in hopes it will be the avenue you pursue. Begin this new attitude now. It is never too late.

Since divorce does not seem to be a fad which will fade anytime soon, there needs to be a "better divorce" guide. And I am here to add my two cents worth. (Since I charge over $200 and hour, that means you will be getting approximately 37 seconds of my expertise.)

But wait, there's more. Not only am I an experienced, excellent source of hired gun experience, I have also been a party to a divorce action. Yes, divorce has even affected me. It changed my family. It caused an enormous upheaval for me and for my daughter. It was one, if not, the most difficult times of my life. But it taught me compassion and, out of necessity, it caused me to look at divorce differently.

My qualifications for authoring this manuscript are not just based on legal theories or courtroom expertise. The following is not legal advice. It is common sense advice. It is based on my personal experience, as well as on actions and reactions of people, friends, clients, and family members who have been touched by this divorce tidal wave. It is a "please consider this point of view before you completely obliterate the other side" guide. It is not a "how to win a divorce by force and coercion" guide. Let me share an inside secret with you…no one wins in a divorce, (except maybe the attorneys). No one wins.

You may not want the divorce, but it is up to you to redefine the outcome of your situation. It is not just for the present. A divorce with children is never over. There is never a winner. But if the situation is not handled fairly and appropriately now, there can be losers. What do we call the losers? Your children.

My personal life has allowed me to experience most of the emotions I refer to in this book. I was divorced when our daughter was three. I did not want the divorce. I was a single working mother with a small child and very little money. There were times I could do nothing but cry and cuss. My experience had taught me how to maneuver in a divorce situation, yet I was completely lost. I was not logical or objective. I could not see past the swollen red nose on my face. I remember arguing with my soon to be ex-husband about our refrigerator. I can still remember his comment when I demanded the appliance.

"You know, our relationship is going to last a lot longer than this refrigerator. It is only a refrigerator. It isn't that important. You take it."

It was only a refrigerator. That one statement set the tone for how I have dealt with the subject of divorce, and my clients, from that time forward. Although my husband was a real poop-head for wanting the divorce, he was an exceptionally wise poop-head. He saw the *big picture*.

Our story turned out to be a happy one. We have raised our daughter together. We have been and will always be her immediate family. A divorce does not stop you from being a family. It just redefines the roles of each participant. You decide how that will affect your children. For better…or worse. (Isn't that supposed to be in the marriage vows, not the divorce definitions?)

My ex-husband is one of my favorite people. I have chosen to remember and continue to see his good traits. My daughter knows I care very much for him, and therefore, she has never had to choose between us. If you project your dislike for the other parent, children will feel as if they must choose between you. It will tear them in two if you consciously, or subconsciously, expose them to such negative emotions. You will definitely not be considering the *bigger picture* if your children suffer from such destructive actions.

I am currently married to a wonderful man, who also happens to be divorced. We have dealt with his children, his ex-wife, his ex-wife's family, her spouse, her spouse's family…well, you get the idea. We have a son together, my daughter, his two daughters, six grandchildren, a son he has from another relationship ten years into our marriage, three dogs, three cats, and a Partridge in a pear tree. It is complicated and at times messy. However, we have weathered this blended family, redefined roles and many times gritted our teeth. We have forced ourselves to see the *big picture*. That is the key to sanity.

My many professional experiences have led me to realize that most people go blindly into a marriage, a divorce and a remarriage without appropriate tools. Because of this lack of knowledge and options, they respond with inappropriate actions, which may negatively affect their lives for many years to come. My personal experience has allowed me to empathize with the participants and understand their pain, but realize you can turn a tough situation into a positive outcome with the right attitude and choices.

These dual roles have given me an insight into the national epidemic labeled "divorce," a topic that must be re-addressed, redefined, and approached in a more appropriate manner.

I daily see the pain that divorce causes and I have experienced it first hand. I offer these suggestions and recommendations hoping to soothe the pain, if only a little. None of these suggestions should be followed blindly, but taken as guidelines to help you through this difficult time. Hopefully, you will glean some common sense from this book, and use this "sense" to be able to take charge of the situation. One must attempt to see the *bigger picture* of life as well as divorce. One must be aware of available options and different approaches to this transition in life, as it is one of the most emotionally and financially traumatic situations anyone can go through.

This book offers ten suggestions to help you through the maze of divorce. It will provide step-by-step advice on how to have a fair, sane (or as sane as possible) divorce, and how to handle most situations arising out of any divorce, as well as post divorce problems. While many areas in this book deal directly with children, it will also provide valuable information to couples without them.

The advice and recommendations I give in this book are not to be taken as legal advice. These suggestions are based on the 28-plus years of listening to every possible divorce scenario in the universe, living through a personal divorce, seeing both good and bad divorces, and just using common sense, (a sense you immediately lose when in this position). So let's begin negotiating the divorce obstacle course.

SUGGESTION #1

Don't Get Married!

A close friend of mine once declared, "The first step to divorce is marriage." As cynical as this seems, most people don't contemplate this possible outcome during their courtship. But consider this, if we didn't have one, we wouldn't have the other, and I'd be unemployed (and happily looking for another profession).

Obviously, if you picked up this book you must be at least considering divorce, which means you have already ignored the first premise of this book. Although you may feel this recommendation is somewhat belated, I would still like to share a few important thoughts.

You need to review the life choices you've made and filter this difficult time through the lens of marriage. I suggest you spend some time concentrating on the fact that you did choose marriage and, more importantly, marriage to this one special person. Since you are actually perusing this book, probably standing in the self-help aisle of your favorite bookstore, you are obviously considering the "D" word and you need to view decisions you make through the lens of the marriage. If you aren't considering the "D" word, put this book back in its proper place and run, don't walk, to the travel section and plan a long needed trip.

But since you are standing here browsing through these pages, I'm assuming you must have chosen marriage. Further, if you are considering or proceeding with a divorce you quite possibly have no money at all, let alone excess money for a vacation. So stay away from the travel aisle, buy this book and be prepared to be exposed to some different ideas and thoughts. It is very difficult, but you need to view your present circumstances as objectively as possible to be able to proceed through this time in your life.

Everyone going through a divorce has made at least one conscious decision, the decision to get married. If you have children, obviously another conscious decision was made! (Okay, so some of you out there were unconscious at the time of conception or the children were a huge surprise, but nonetheless you knew how babies were made.)

Long before you arrived at divorce court, you made numerous choices. You need to understand you will be living with the consequences of these choices for a long time. These are your decisions and you need to own them. You chose to marry this person and, in many cases, chose to have children with them. Keep these decisions in mind as you read all the other suggestions found within.

I have clients come to me demanding that I do something to keep their spouse out of their lives and out of their children's lives during or after a divorce. Let me emphasize if you have children together, you are joined at the hip forever and the sooner you accept this, the sooner the damage control can begin.

"What did you say? Damage control? Wait a minute, I want you to solve and fix everything in the next 10 minutes, not just control the damage."

Sorry, that is truly the only thing a divorce attorney can do to help in this situation...control the damage of a broken marriage. Divorce does not fix anything. It may solve a certain set of problems but all you are doing is trading one set of problems for another. The question to ask is, "Which problems are the most difficult to control, the ones in the marriage, or the ones arising from divorce?" Marriage may not be forever, but just remember, divorce is! Let me reiterate that fact again, divorce is forever and will affect all aspects of your future.

The problems in a marriage are as varied as the people in each relationship. They may be infidelity, financial, sexual, or philosophical. Other than emotional trauma, the problems arising out of a divorce without children are mostly financial. The problems of paying bills, having to sell property, keeping your credit scores unaffected because of joint debts are all ongoing, and concerns that do not go away overnight. If may take many years to correct the financial problems a divorce causes.

However, the problems in a divorce with children are more intense, harder to define, let alone solve, and may never be totally resolved (without of course, buying this book and paying specific attention to details mentioned throughout). But, in actuality, some problems may never be completely settled. While the financial concerns are most often magnified tenfold, the emotional aspects now not only deal with you, but also with the most precious property you possess, your children. Remember, you do not solve problems with a divorce; you trade them in for different ones. Make sure you are aware of this axiom.

Let's go back Suggestion # 1. Don't get married, as marriage is the breeding ground for divorce. Not a happy thought, but definitely a reality in today's society. Before you exchange vows, you should make it a priority to objectively view this person's basic qualities of fairness, honesty and integrity. If your spouse had these positive traits before your marriage, chances are they will continue after the "I do's," and into the "I don'ts" even if temporarily hidden beneath the surface. If they didn't have them before the marriage, no attorney in the world can change your spouse's basic personality traits. In fact, a divorce will probably exacerbate them.

Although love is blind, it would have been helpful to put on your glasses of objectivity and analyze your true love's personality traits before you tied the knot. (I sound like your mother, don't I?) As you are going through a separation, remember this person is the one you still have to deal with.

Recent divorce statistics indicate that a first marriage has a 60% change of ending in divorce. If your spouse is fair, then either the marriage has a much better chance of survival, or if divorce becomes a reality, it too will hopefully be fair. Literally considering what reaction your spouse may have to this unfortunate scenario is definitely a prudent exercise prior to the wedding.

Now, if everyone adhered to Suggestion #1, and didn't marry (obviously I have broken it twice), our society would be substantially altered. It would greatly hamper our procreation, and place a real crunch in the bridal boutique business, not to mention also running divorce attorneys out of business.

If you did not adhere to this very simple rule, and are now reading this book, you are probably either going through the most traumatic time of your life, both financially and emotionally, or seriously considering doing so. Now you know why the first suggestion is so practical.

However, if you objectively picked a good partner that passed the "divorce" test with flying colors and you still end up in divorce court, at least you should have a much easier time at this juncture in your life. You may now just skim the rest of this book.

On the other hand, you may also find that your judgment was absolutely horrible, aliens have taken over your spouse's body, or that you married Godzilla. Obviously, that is why there is more than one chapter in this book, so read on.

One more thought regarding the institution of marriage. Contrary to my obviously somewhat callused outlook, I do believe very strongly in marriage. I do not believe in divorce, even though I am divorced, married to a divorced man, and make my living wading through the corpses of the divorced masses. I trust my experiences can serve as some type of a road map to get you going in the right direction and that you will ultimately decide to stay in your marriage. If that is not possible, then I sincerely hope my comments will make the divorce as positive a situation as possible.

Marriage should be taken very seriously and divorce should not be considered as an easy option. Marriage should be seen as a badge of honor, a commitment, a statement of your integrity. At about this time you are saying to yourself, "But I thought she was divorced. She obviously isn't a pillar of virtue."

Maybe my mistakes can become lessons for others. Although, my first marriage ended in divorce, we remain friends to this day and have raised a wonderful daughter. It can be done. The point is...*if you can't stay married; strive to have a good divorce.*

One additional thought. I would like you to keep a few mental "snap shots" of the happy times during your marriage. For example, visualize the day you were married, the day your child was born, happy vacations you enjoyed together. Remember the reasons you liked your spouse, such as how he cleaned up the dog vomit without you asking, or how she didn't laugh when you put "Grecian formula" on your rapidly graying hair. Keep these close to your heart and top of mind when you are negotiating the legal ramifications of your divorce. These thoughts may hurt, but they should also help you seek a solution that is fair to both of you.

To review. (Did I mention that you will be tested later?)

1. Don't get married.
2. Don't marry someone unless you could be happily divorced from them.
3. Don't get married without a very firm commitment to grit your teeth and get through the bad times.
4. Remember the good times.

SUGGESTION #2

Don't Get Divorced!

Half of my readers are now pining, "But I don't want the divorce!" while the other half are saying, "Mind your own business, you don't know what's best for me!" Unfortunately, divorce may now appear to be imminent whether you want it or not. One of you may feel betrayed. One of you may feel impatient. Either way, decisions must be made.

Since divorce is a reality affecting the future of both spouses, both should strive to view this tragedy as fairly as possible. But what does divorce really mean? Simply put, a divorce is comprised of two concerns: First, it is a financial dissolution. Second, it makes provisions regarding children...Period. Legally, that's it. However, because emotions are so overwhelming, it is often very difficult to even get to the point where you can make intelligent decisions regarding these two issues. Take your time. Be kind to yourself and to the other spouse. There is, in all probability, a waiting period for the divorce to be final. There are different reasons for this, but the one to be aware of is this; you need time to heal, to review, to hope and to decide. Be patient. Be kind. Be aware. But be smart. Don't make decisions until you have as much information as possible.

This will be a very short chapter, as I am sure you are tired of taking advice from somebody who doesn't follow it. However, if there is absolutely, positively, any way to avoid a divorce, I would recommend stretching your imagination, and patience, as far as possible.

I continually recommend counseling to my clients, and my standard speech includes, "Our first priority is to get you two back together, if possible. The last thing we need in this society is another divorce.

However, if there is no way this marriage will work, our next priority is to be as fair and reasonable as possible, so both sides remain friends."

What, you say? Remain friends? Where is the, "ripping his throat out?" What happened to "putting a contract out on his life?" Where is the provisions about "taking him/her to the cleaners?"

Although these responses are very understandable and extremely frequent, avoid bitterness at all possible junctures since it truly doesn't accomplish anything. Also, and let me be very clear, avoid attorneys who suggest these types of antics, for they are paving the road for a very difficult and costly divorce. An attorney who is assertive, yet fair, and will not allow the other side to take advantage of you is the best possible partner you can have.

But, of course, that advice is only if you are getting a divorce. Since you blatantly broke Suggestion #1, hopefully by following Suggestion #2 you will never have to read the rest of this interesting and thought-provoking manual! However, if you are still considering divorce, consider the following.

A study by the University of Chicago appearing in the 2002 summer issue of "Prevention Magazine," found that many couples considering divorce can, in fact, repair their relationships. Of the 700 ready-to-split couples studied, research revealed that two-thirds of those who stayed married were happy five years later. The couples endured the many difficult problems, (including alcoholism, infidelity, financial hardships and serious illness), by being stubbornly committed, working together on issues and lowering expectations, researchers said. (An exception to this was relationships where physical violence was present and divorce was usually a better option in these cases. I will discuss this topic in more detail later.)

If you wish to try to be a positive statistic as outlined in the above paragraph, do go to a marriage counselor. It may take some time to find one you both like. If you don't like the first one, try others. Ask around. Ask your minister for a referral. Ask the best divorce attorney in town for a referral. (Believe me; they will know a gross of counselors.) Seek out this individual early on, especially before you can't stand being in the same room as Godzilla. However, you do need "two to tango," and sometimes, actually quite often, one party won't participate. If this happens, counseling for one may still help immensely.

Steven Covey, author of the book *The Seven Habits of Highly Effective People*, an optimistic and thought provoking directive on a happier and more productive life, writes about an experience he had after a speaking engagement. The topic involved marriage and how it fit within his overall philosophy. Shortly after his speech, a man approached him and related that although he was married, he no longer loved his wife. How, he wondered, could he incorporate the seven habits into his impending divorce?

Mr. Covey relates how he told him not to get divorced but to go home and 'love his wife.' This response astounded the man and he questioned whether or not Mr. Covey heard him correctly. Mr. Covey assured him that his hearing was just fine. He then simply explained that 'love' is an active verb and requires continual reaction. Love is how you respond to your partner including the things you say and do as well as the sacrifices and gifts you make to them. It is not a nebulous emotion that is unrelated to your reality that comes and goes on a whim, with no control from you. Love is something you cultivate and foster. He concluded his response by emphasizing to this gentleman that he had made a commitment to 'love' he wife and he should follow-through with that commitment!

Mr. Covey ended this passage by explaining that many months later this same individual approached him and recanted the above experience. He related that he went home and consciously tried to follow the advice he had been given although in his heart he was only doing it to alleviate his guilt and prove Mr. Covey wrong. To his surprise, his wife started responding differently to him, and in turn he also felt his emotions growing for her. He explained that he and his wife were still married and very happy. Actively practicing Mr. Covey's philosophy of 'love is an action verb,' made all the difference.

Try it. Love the person you made a commitment to and do so actively. Remember the old hippie theme song… "Love the one you're with?" Try it.

(I have been a fan of Steven Covey's for some time. I offer my sincere apologies to him for paraphrasing the above heart-warming story but I think you'll agree this anecdote is very appropriate to Suggestion#2. I recommend Mr. Covey's books often and couples who are experiencing difficulty with their relationship may find his marriage philosophies very helpful.)

Additionally, when attempting to stay married, sometimes it's simply best to have a very short memory. If your spouse has done something atrocious (left the cap off the toothpaste, doesn't know how to turn on the vacuum, had an affair with his bimbo secretary, or even gotten somebody pregnant), try to forget it and move on with your lives. Once again, counseling at this juncture will probably be helpful, if not mandatory.

As I related in the introduction, my second marriage has weathered a straying husband, and a child as a result of that affair. As you can imagine this was a very difficult time for me personally, but we had both been through a divorce and knew first hand the problems arising from a broken relationship. Additionally, we had a five year old son and knew what a divorce can do to a child. We also knew that in any marriage problems will arise and running away won't stop them. In fact, as I explained earlier, divorce just creates a new and different set of problems. And, if you marry again, your new relationship will most likely have its own difficulties. Try your utmost to define and solve your marital problems now and make 'love an action word' in your lives.

Many of my clients from second marriages profess a very insightful understanding of the problems relating to divorce. They often admit they might still be married to their first spouse had they "known then what they know now." And what, pray tell, is this mystical knowledge that they now know? Simply, all marriages have problems, go through bad times, and are not always fun or easy. But guess what...divorce is not easy either, as these clients will attest.

There is also a reality in divorce involving the children which must also be addressed. The facts are these: mom is now a part time mother and dad, a part time father. Your children will only have each of you a portion of their lives. I don't care if you are the primary parent or not, you will lose out on so many of your children's precious moments after a divorce. You will have only one-half the holidays, one-half the weekends, one-half the smiles, the tears, the talks. If you think that you'll get divorced, get custody of the kids and go on as usual, think again. You will lose out on a huge portion of their lives.

I struggled to accept the fact my child was going to live a splintered life, bouncing back and forth, week to week, holiday to holiday, never feeling completely at peace. The fact that one parent is always gone leaves a child feeling incomplete. If you consider nothing else, this fact alone should help you forget and forgive the blemishes of your marriage. It helped me understand that properly motivated almost every marriage can work. What better motivation than your precious child?

One more word of advice. Do not have an affair. If you are, stop it! Go to counseling and recommit to your spouse and make 'love' an active verb. I don't know actual statistics, but my professional experience reflects that affairs are over almost as soon as the marriage is. They don't work. They are destructive.

However, the one absolute exception to the rule of forgiving and forgetting is physical, emotional, or verbal abuse. Do not accept any physical abuse from your spouse. Do not allow emotional or mental abuse to continue, either. If you spouse continually has affairs and is unwilling to change, I suggest this is also a form of abuse and must not be tolerated.

Any abuse is unacceptable and must be dealt with immediately and professionally. Contact your local mental health facility, the YWCA, your minister, or a friend at the first sign of trouble. Document the abuse with police reports, photographs, diaries, visits to the doctor, or just confiding to the friend. Get help. There is a better life, for both you and your children. The local battered women's shelter is an amazing resource. They will give you all the information you need to prepare for an independent life. There are many people who will help you get there but you must take the first step. The statistics show it takes 6-8 attempts to leave an abusive situation before one is successful. If you, or someone you are close to, are in a destructive situation, please don't allow yourself or them to go through the six or eight trial runs. Equally important, if not more so, don't let your children think this kind of relationship is acceptable or they will emulate it later in life. There are options. You are strong.

Take divorce very seriously and know that it will affect your life and the lives of your children for a long, long time. If however, you are involved in a divorce for whatever reason, take heart, for you can and will live through it. You can have a better life in the future even if the divorce was not of your choosing. What you do from now on will be based on the choices you make, and you can choose to have a wonderful life.

Do not let your spouse make you feel bad about yourself. Eleanor Roosevelt once said that no one can ever make you feel inferior without your consent. Do not give them that consent. You are a worthy and strong individual and you will come out of the divorce a better person.

To review:

1. Have a short memory.
2. Go to counseling early and often.
3. Don't get divorced unless all other options, including amnesia, have been ruled out.

SUGGESTION #3

Don't Hire Perry Mason

Okay, so you find yourself facing a possible divorce and reading this book to hopefully find some answers to your dilemma. Now what can you do?

Choosing a divorce lawyer is probably your next step. It is one of the most important decisions you will make during this tremendously emotional time in which you now find yourself.

The attorney sets the tone of the divorce and can either make it as amicable, or as horrific, as possible. Attorneys who have a reputation for annihilating the other side in a divorce case may be very tempting at this time of your life, but avoid this temptation no matter what! They will do nothing but run up your fees, polarize the participants, and quite possible cause rifts between the parties that may never be healed.

This does not mean, however, to hire a piece of cooked spaghetti. You need a strong, assertive and knowledgeable attorney. You need to ask around, visit the courtroom, interview attorneys, call the local Bar (the Bar Association for Lawyers—not the neighborhood pub) and ask for referrals.

Hire an attorney who primarily practices within the field of Family Law and is involved in related bar committees, etc. Feel comfortable with your choice and trust your instincts. Pick an attorney that is respected and successful. They are successful for a reason. Don't hire the cheapest attorney as you will most likely get what you pay for.

There are many financial and personal concerns that must be addressed now, or you may very possibly never be able to deal with them again. Having a good lawyer right out of the chute is essential.

Here is a checklist that can help you hire the appropriate attorney for your needs.

1. Ask friends and relatives for referrals. Attend a support group for recently divorced people and ask the members who they would, and would not, recommend.
2. Call the local Bar Association and ask for referrals of attorneys who regularly practice in the area of Family Law.
3. Look in the yellow pages for attorneys. Search for those with Family Law, Divorce, and Domestic Law as their primary area(s) of emphasis.
4. Go to court and watch different attorneys practice in the courtroom. Ask for business cards.
5. Call the Family Law Judge's clerk and ask for a list of divorce mediators. Call these mediators and ask what attorneys they would recommend.
6. Ask a psychologist or counselor for a recommendation as they often work with attorneys during divorce actions.
7. Do not price shop and hire the cheapest attorney. Once again, you get what you pay for. (I am reminded of an old wooden sign tacked to a telephone pole near a small, rundown strip center several miles from my home. In hand-painted letters the message reads…"Divorces and Bankruptcies—$35." Now that's a deal!)
8. Call the referred attorneys for a screening interview over the phone. Are they friendly yet professional?
9. Ask the following questions: Do you offer a free initial consultation, at least on the phone? How long have you practiced law? Are you a member of a local or state bar association and do you serve on any domestic law-related committees? Do you have a Martindale-Hubble rating? (I realize you have no idea what this is, but if they don't either, hang up quickly)
10. If you like them on the phone and if they have answered questions thoroughly but succinctly, make an appointment for a personal interview. This may cost at least an hour of the

attorneys' time, but it will be well worth your time and money to make sure you are selecting the right one.

11. During this interview, ask for their rates and how they bill. Affirm that you will get an account of all the time spent and costs expensed. Remember, the only thing an attorney has to sell is time, so all contact with them will be recorded and billed.
12. An experienced attorney will inform you that nothing you are divulging is confidential until they have actually been retained by you. Resist telling them your life story until you have actually retained them.
13. A retainer is money paid to your attorney upon accepting your case and is very normal. This fee is a prepayment of time needed to prepare for your case and represent you completely.
14. It is important to have a good feeling about your attorney. Do they shake your hand, seem friendly and communicate with you easily? Do they have a nice, professional office? (It doesn't need to be opulent, but it should feel comfortable and definitely not snotty.) Obviously, the rule of thumb is the nicer the offices, the more successful the tenant. That should be taken as a clue to their competency.
15. Finally, hire an attorney as soon as possible after you know you will be going through a divorce.

Once you hire an attorney, here are a few rules to follow that will help you communicate effectively, prepare the case, and hopefully keep your costs down.

1. Whining never makes your points any clearer. In fact, it just makes life noisier, you more obnoxious, and your bill larger. Try to stay as focused as possible.
2. Unless it's an emergency, jot down questions or problems as they rear their little ugly heads, and only make one phone call per week, instead of two…or three…or ten per day.
3. The attorney cannot make your spouse disappear, quit dating that new bimbo in his life, have a complete personality change, pay child support exactly on the day it's due, make your mother-in-law more tolerable (remember, you didn't like her

before the divorce), make the divorce go away, or mend your broken heart.

4. The attorney can:
    a. Answer your questions promptly, professionally, and with compassion.
    b. Return your phone calls promptly.
    c. Know what options are available for specific legal problems such as noncompliance with a temporary order, late payment of child support, etc, and allow you to make an informed decision on what to do.
    d. Discover as much as possible about your financial matters in a reasonable time for a reasonable fee.
    e. Deal with the other side in a professional and timely manner.
    f. Send you to mediation, and know when it can and can't work.
    g. Propose appropriate settlements that are fair to all in a timely fashion.
    h. Be the initiator in all negotiations.

Something you can do to help with the litigation is to send letters or e-mails to your attorney with concerns, facts, and overviews of your case. These can be filed and answered when appropriate. You can also do a lot of your own legwork like obtaining your own bank statements, mortgage records, pension plan records, income tax returns and business documents. Provide your attorney with a list of things you feel would be beneficial for them to obtain that you're unable to locate. An attorney will be glad to do all these things for you, but it will obviously result in higher fees.

Keep a diary of important concerns that happen during the proceedings, especially the dates you have children. Include a thorough, but succinct, overview of your concerns and questions and make a time that the attorney can address each concern to your satisfaction.

Our review:

1. Don't hire a mercenary.

2. Do your research and feel comfortable with whom you do hire.
3. Don't whine…it costs money.
4. Respect your attorneys' time, as it is literally your money.

SUGGESTION #4

Don't Get Mad—Get Even

To understand this chapter, we must first define the terms. The definition of "even" in the dictionary is "equal, fair, leaving nothing due on either side." Some definitions of "mad" are: crazy, insane, illogical, carried away by intense anger, completely unrestrained by reason or judgment." Hum…which of these concepts would be better to follow when your entire future lies in the balance? You would be surprised at the answer. However, in case you were wondering, the correct answer is 'even.' This is an essential point that must be made at the beginning of your divorce. Everyone needs to be fair in all aspects of the process.

Contrary to my prior advice to stay married at almost any cost, and knowing that making a decision to move forward with your divorce is difficult, it is better to leave your marriage while you are both still friends with some mutual respect still in place. If there is so much hatred and history of bad feelings in the relationship that it is impossible to even communicate, this chapter will be hard to follow. There is a fine line in a marriage when deciding how much is "enough" and yet be able to maintain a friendship. However, let me emphasize that the main ingredient in a tolerable divorce is amicable communication between all parities.

I was lucky enough to be divorced from my first husband while we still cared for each other. In fact, we have a better relationship now than we did most of our married life. I attribute this entirely to three things: (1) At the time of divorce, we still liked each other; (2) We were fair and treated each other with respect; (3) Most importantly, we both knew the other cherished our daughter. I also found I had followed my advice from Suggestion #1—I had chosen a mate with integrity.

If any one of these attributes (liking and respecting your spouse, and mutual love of a child) can be nurtured, you can have a 'good' divorce and you may throw this book away. (After, of course, you've paid for it).

The key ingredient in staying friendly during this period is to treat the other person fairly and with respect. This situation epitomizes what God had in mind when he said, "Do unto others as you would have them do unto you." I realize this can be an extremely difficult request, especially if your heart is broken and your spouse is vacationing in Tierra del Fuego with a new found love.

I am not saying you have to condone, or even accept, your spouse's actions. I am saying, however, you need to be financially and emotionally fair in the legal aspects of your action. If not, the drain on you both financially and emotionally will be overwhelming. Hate only eats up the person doing the hating. Hate fuels law suits and in the long run only succeeds in lining your attorney's pockets. (I thought that last one would get you attention.)

Obviously, the anger and hurt do need to be dealt with, especially if there are children in the relationship. Counselors, ministers and friends are there to help you deal with these issues. However, your attorney, and especially your children should not be relied upon to do so.

How do you stay fair and balanced? Unless you are Fox news and need no suggestions, I offer the following ideas.

Do not vow to take every penny your spouse has. Do not threaten to keep the children from them. Do not attempt to use legal means to punish your spouse. Do not try to manipulate the children. And do not, under any circumstance, say anything derogatory about your spouse to the children.

Let me repeat this rule. Do not, under any circumstances, say anything negative about your spouse to the children. Your goal may be to wound your spouse by "showing the children" what a horrible person he/she is. You may be attempting to turn the children against him/her and justify your position through negative comments. Or, you may simply be venting your emotions and are unaware of just how destructive your statements are. Stop it. Stop it. Stop it. You are wounding your children immensely.

You would never allow anyone in the world to hurt your children, but you would be injuring them more than any stranger ever could. Negative comments concerning their other parent will literally destroy them. When these verbal attacks occur, they are forced to either agree this person is a louse or they will mentally, if not verbally defend them, and thus appear be attacking you. Can you say, "Lose-Lose"?

Now, as no other time in their lives, they need a safe haven, a place they can be themselves, and not be forced to take sides. They need to be nurtured and feel secure. They need to know both parents love them. They need to know that it is okay to love both parents and both sides of the family. They need to know this divorce is not their fault. They need to see their parents as still their parents, and not forced to be allies in the divorce war. Be fair to your children.

You may not always be your spouses' mate, but your spouse will always be your child's parent. Read that sentence again. And again. You may not always be married, but you will always be your child's family. That means you will always be your spouses' family, connected by your children. A divorce is not a normal lawsuit, where at the end of the litigation both parties go their own way and never see each other again. A divorce is a continuation of a relationship, the family relationship, (albeit restructured), and must continue to be treated with respect.

Believe me, if you make a concerted effort to be friends and be fair when it comes to your children, the other spouse will most likely reciprocate in kind.

This same philosophy of fairness applies when it comes to dividing assets and debts, which incidentally also affects your children. Fair, however, does not always mean easy especially if communications have broken down. You may have to fight for "fair" if the other side is not being fair. Many times "appropriate confrontation" is needed to obtain an "appropriate settlement".

Some clients are afraid of conflict and would rather give up than "go to the mats." When I have a client that is ready to throw in the proverbial towel because their spouse is acting like a "weenie" (a legalistic term for not being fair), I strongly recommend they think this decision through and understand their options.

Knowing whether or not to be assertive, yet reasonable, during this critical thought process is exactly what your attorney is paid to do. Allow me to paraphrase a hypothetical conversation I would have in this situation.

"Right now giving in (or giving up) may seem the easiest solution. And who knows…it might be. However, it is probably not the best solution for you under the circumstances. In six months, or six years, you will be kicking yourself (as well as me) if we don't approach this divorce for what it is—a dissolution of a financial partnership. You have only one shot to divide assets and debts equally and, if necessary, insure the appropriate and fair redistribution of income. And that shot is now. Do not be afraid to go to trial, if required, for a fair and equitable outcome."

Allow me a few more "Do Nots." Do not confuse and or connect this financial discussion with decisions regarding the custody and/or visitation of your children. Do not use the children as hostages to get a better financial settlement. For instance, do not say, "I will go after custody if you don't do things my way." Or, "I won't let you see the children unless I get my way financially."

You would rather die than see your children hurt, yet you would be amazed how many parents injure their children emotionally by exploiting them as blackmail fodder without ever blinking an eye. Do not let your spouse attempt to extort assets by using your children. The vast majority of the time your spouse will either back down, or the courts will see through their veiled attempts at blackmail and not allow it.

Please remember this…there is no such thing as justice, only an attempt at justice. What you think is "just," your spouse, Godzilla, thinks is horrendous. Obviously, both sides to a dispute rarely feel justice has been served, as neither side gets everything they requested.

Also, please closely consider and remember this. A divorce, especially a divorce with children, is not a win/lose situation. It is first a financial dissolution and next a redefinition of the family. Although the *marriage relationship* is dissolved, your *family relationship* continues, just under a different set of ground rules. Keep remembering the Kodak moments of the family; first birthday parties, summer vacations, Christmas mornings, and other happy times while you are negotiating your settlement.

Be fair to your children. But also remember, what is fair in regards to your children may or may not be what you or your spouse wants. Listen to your attorney and your children, but most of all listen to a counselor if needed.

When considering your assets, fair can be very subjective at times. Start by compiling a spread sheet of both assets and debts, factoring in earning ability of both spouses. Definitely take the advice of your attorney during this process to insure you are considering all aspects.

Consult counselors to determine what is "fair" for the children and consider that their ages make an immense difference when it comes to parenting time. The "best interest of the children" must be considered first and foremost before "fair" to the parents can be factored in.

Review:

1. If your divorce is imminent, get out while you still care about each other.
2. Be fair, regardless of how the other side acts.
3. Be fair to your children and keep them out of the middle.
4. Never equate fair with revenge.
5. When evaluating fairness, trust your instincts first, and then the advice of your attorney.

SUGGESTION #5

Never Forget That You Are Still Family

Emotions are quite possibly the most difficult obstacles to overcome in a divorce. If your scenario involves a mutual parting of the ways, this suggestion will be much easier to follow. However, if either party feels abandoned, guilty, misused or betrayed, it is extremely difficult to put these feelings on the back burner when addressing the issue of your children. But you must because your children's future depends on it.

After you have come to terms with the fact that divorce is inevitable, please follow this guide as soon as possible.

1. Sit down together and tell your children about the divorce.
2. Carefully explain that this decision had nothing to do with them and they are definitely not at fault.
3. Let them know there is nothing they can do to change this decision.
4. Emphasize that their parents have difficulty getting along and it is simply no one person's fault. (Okay, I know you want to scream, "It is someone's fault, because if he/she had (insert one—quit drinking, quit seeing the bimbo, quit gambling the savings, quit picking his nose, quit nagging, we wouldn't be here. But don't give in to the anger. Don't discuss any reasons.)
5. Tell them you, as their parents, will handle this problem. It is not their responsibility.

6. Emphasize that you are both still their mom and dad, you love them with all your hearts, and you will always be a family, only in a different way.
7. Briefly outline a possible schedule and time frame of which kids need to be aware. (A timetable should include things such as when someone is moving out, when they will see that parent again, when parenting time will be, etc.)
8. Answer all their questions about the future as much as you possibly can, but absolutely minimize answers to the past and what happened between their parents.
9. Assure them everything will work out, but acknowledge that things will be different and harder than usual at times.
10. Be honest. Tell them it's okay to be sad, it's okay and expected to love both parents, that money may be tight but manageable, etc.
11. Do not place blame and definitely do not let your children place blame.
12. And finally, understand that this will probably be the most difficult conversation you will ever initiate during your life.

After this discussion and the actual events take place, (divorce filed, parent moves out, new second home for the kids), give them ample time to adjust. Don't change anything that doesn't absolutely need to be changed. Keep them in their normal routine as much as possible—same home, same school, same friends, etc.

And for goodness sake, and here's the big one, do not introduce a "significant other" into their lives for at least three to six months. If this "significant other" was the primary instigation of the divorce, this rule is even more important! Trust me on this one. If introduced too soon, the betrayed parent will overreact (and I personally think has a right to), while the "erring parent" is simply attempting to have this person accepted immediately in order to ease their guilt. The kids do not need this agitation in their lives immediately following the tremendous upheaval of divorce. Children need to feel comfortable and secure when they are with their parents, and introducing a new element into an already unstable and uncomfortable situation is one burden they do not need to bear at this time. There will be plenty of time down the road to introduce this new relationship so please be patient.

However, on the other hand, if there has been some time since the separation and the children seem to be reacting appropriately to the situation, do not throw a total fit if your divorcing spouse introduces the children to this new "friend." After all, to include this new person in the lives of the children is only natural.

It is a reality that there will be new relationships in the lives of both parents and, in fact, this is healthy. It means the parent is healing and moving on with life. It also doesn't hurt the children to have other people in their lives who care for them. However, this new "significant other" must know the role they are to play. It is the role of a stepparent and definitely not one of a parent.

It is extremely important for the children to feel like they have a permanent home at both mom and dad's as soon after the divorce as possible. Make sure there are enough rooms where they can relax and feel welcome. Also, ensure each child has a space to call their own. If finances prevent a separate bedroom, find a special area in the bedroom they share or make accommodations in another room where they can keep their personal treasures.

If you can emotionally handle it, celebrate major events in the children's lives with the other parent and families. Have a birthday party and invite all extended family members. Everyone should go to the special programs and cheer embarrassingly, attend parent teacher conferences together, be present when they go on their first date etc. My point is simply this—the decisions you make will allow your child to feel the love, warmth and praise your child deserves from both of you during life's many celebrations. Be supportive and be involved!

On the other hand, if the two of you find it difficult to be kind and civil to each other, nix this idea immediately. Stay away from conflict in front of your children at all costs. Either take turns going to the functions or sit in opposite corners. Make sure the kids know its okay to talk with both sets of parents. The most stressful thing a child will experience is to have both parents in the same proximity and not know what to do, whom to talk to or whom it would offend. Please do not put them in this position. Please allow them to love both of you.

Contact the in-laws (or at this stage you may refer to them as out-laws) immediately after the divorce proceedings and let them know their involvement in your children's lives will continue to be important.

Do this even if they refuse to acknowledge your existence and treat you as if you are invisible. It's hard to fight when one party refuses to participate…so don't participate. Let them know you still care about them and will do everything possible to foster a relationship with their grandchildren, nieces, nephews, etc.

In-laws may initially react defensively and automatically assume you may try to control the relationship or interfere. Both time and your positive approach will prove them wrong. Let them know how important they are to your children and will always be welcome in your home. As difficult as you may think this will be, I guarantee that offering an olive branch is a tremendous benefit for your children, and the kindness will return to you tenfold.

If you can't bring yourself to say this to them in person, write them a nice letter. (Yes Virginia, people used to write letters before computers were invented!) Make sure you do not bring them into your divorce, say anything negative about anybody, tell them your side of the story, try to make them take sides, or give them ground rules they must follow. The one exception is they are also expected to not say anything negative about anyone in front of the children.

Until she passed away, I sent my ex-mother-in-law flowers on her birthday, Mothers Day, and Christmas. She was very special to my daughter, and therefore, to me.

Little things like a call or a card now and then will let them know you were sincere when you indicated your desire to keep that special relationship going. Even though you may not receive a response from them immediately, or for many years, you should continue to foster this relationship for you children's sake. Remember, your attitudes and opinions rub off on your children, even if they remain unspoken. In the long run, your children will have a much healthier relationship with their family and thus with everyone. Your example of being kind, fair and involved in other's lives is a huge opportunity for them to learn from, and someday emulate, your actions.

Children suffer immensely when their parents divorce. Do not add additional pain by denying them access to loved ones and loving situations. Make their lives as loving and loved as possible. It is the best present you can give them.

And finally, in a loving family, people work out their differences. There will inevitably be times of disagreement and conflict. Get counseling. Attend mediation sessions. See a minister together. But do not, I repeat, do not go back to court unless all other avenues have failed.

A quick recap:

1. Approach the divorce as a family.
2. Allow the children to love and be loved by all members of the family.
3. Stay in touch with the in-laws.
4. Be sincere and respectful in your actions.
5. Get a calling card and use it.
6. Stay out of court!

SUGGESTION #6

Don't Get Jealous—Get Zealous

There are two overwhelming concerns one faces during and after a divorce. One is the emotional aspect (Am I going to lose my children's affection, lose control over my life, lose my mind?) and the second is the financial impact (Where the heck am I going to get enough money, to buy Christmas presents, pay child support, pay the mortgage, or just to live?)

Be proactive when faced with these new and trying situations. The best way to deal with the emotions you are feeling is to find as many positive things in your life as possible and then make more. My daughter, who was three when her father and I separated, thought divorce meant you just have a bigger family and therefore get more presents. I tried to show her there were just more people in her life to love and also to love her. I have always stayed friendly to her dad and to his subsequent girlfriends and wife. Why, you ask, would you want to do that? Because of my darling daughter.

Her father has always been welcome for holidays and birthdays, either alone or with his new family. My daughter knows that we care about and respect each other and she never feels torn or threatened when we are both around. She has been given the unspoken emotional permission to love us both and feel comfortable at both homes. This allows her to share all aspects of her life with both parents, and to be herself in both worlds. They may be extremely different worlds but they both belong to your children now and you need to accept and respect this. That doesn't mean you have to like your former spouse or condone his/her actions, but you must accept his/her role in your child's life. I truly believe your child will love you both more because of this attitude.

One of the first reactions a divorced parent may have is to feel threatened and/or replaced. This is a notorious time for feeling insecure when the ex-spouse begins a relationship. Stay as friendly as possible with the other parent. Don't be accusatory or defensive. Treat them as you would want them to treat you and your new "significant other."

Once it is obvious that a new relationship will be long-term, my advice to mothers and fathers is that the parents and new "stepparent" meet on neutral ground to make introductions and try to develop a positive relationship. (This is probably about the time you suggest I should be committed to the psychiatric ward for advising you to develop a relationship with this new person.) You are all now saying, "I will never talk to that bimbo/bimbette and will never allow him/her to touch my children while I am alive and kicking." I totally understand your viewpoint and personally think that while it may be a reasonable position to take, it is certainly not realistic or productive. It's time to take a deep breath and review your circumstances.

This individual is going to be in your children's lives whether you like it or not. It is much better that they like you and know you respect their situation, than try to torpedo and sabotage every single thing they do with your children. This is especially important for mothers and stepmothers. I guarantee that the stickiest situations I see in post divorce custody battles is when a stepmother enters the picture and attempts to take control.

So think about it…lunch is always cheaper than attorney's fee! If you meet on neutral ground, tell them you are glad they are in the children's lives and that you appreciate their concern and feelings for the children. Also, explain that you know they have the children's best interest at heart and how hard their role as a stepparent is. I promise you they will be much less defensive and will be more open to working together. If you meet before a negative situation arises, (when all parties would obviously be on their guard) you have a much better chance of a positive relationship with the stepparent. If you become a united front concerning what is in the children's best interest, you will not be archenemies where they are concerned. More importantly, your children will not be the basis for a battleground. Communication from the very beginning pays huge dividends down the road.

Be proactive and obtain counseling for everyone and anyone if problems arise. Prevention is worth a pound of cure and discussing problems before they become international incidents can nip many lawsuits in the bud.

Be proactive in your financial life, also. In most jurisdictions, an amount of child support (and alimony if appropriate—your attorney will advise you) is set at the beginning of the divorce proceedings. These amounts are based on income of the parties, number and ages of the children, outstanding bills and ability to pay. Once these initial amounts are set you must live with them, at least temporarily.

This is an extremely difficult time in your life and financial aspects can be especially painful. If you are in a world of hurt monetarily, there are things you can do, as well as things you should not do.

The very first thing you cannot do is cry in front of your children about money. Second, never say, "If your dad would pay child support on time (or at all), we could eat this month." Again, don't say, "If your mom wasn't squeezing me dry with all the child support I have to pay, I could buy you that new bike." And finally, "If your dad would quit gambling and chasing women and make more money, we could afford the new salt and pepper shaker we so desperately need!" Those are the very first things you don't do.

Now that you have vented, what can you do? Get down to business. Sit down and make a budget. Take the last three to four months' checks, put them in categories, and see what you are actually spending. Don't lie to yourself. Make sure you include everything; haircuts, school expenses, once a year payments, charity, etc.

See where you can cut corners. Can you eat out fewer times each month or go to less expensive places? Can you wash some clothing items instead of dry cleaning them? Can you volunteer more at church or charities and cut back the monetary gifts for awhile? Can you cut the kids hair? (If they are over twelve, forget I mentioned this one).

Determine which categories the kids could help with and, if age appropriate, discuss these with them. Do not make them feel guilty or responsible. Make a game of seeing if you can meet the monthly goals for the categories you discussed. When accomplished, don't forget simple rewards like a picnic in the park; make your own ice cream sundaes, or a movie marathon with all old movies, etc.

Try not to make any big changes in either you or your children's lives right now. Minimize your financial obligations if you can; borrow money from relatives if possible; be creative with gifts; have less taken out for taxes; don't contribute to your retirement account right now; and, even shop at an upscale thrift shop sponsored by snooty society types, etc., but try to keep life as stable and normal as possible. Review your income and expenses frequently. Remember, it is financially impossible to live in two houses on the same income you had trouble living with in one house. Assume both parties' standard of living will be affected…expect it, and accept it. Do not feel sorry for yourself and definitely do not bring the kids to the pity party.

If all else fails, you may need to get a part time job, but remember, your kids need you more right now than they need a pair of designer jeans, contrary to what they may say. Try to work the part time job when the other parent has the children, if possible.

If you still cannot make ends meet and you feel your ex-spouse's trips to Acapulco with his secretary are excessive, talk with your attorney. A well documented budget and expense sheet, along with a narrative of what you are doing to conserve money and make more income, is a great exhibit to show the court to increase child support and/or spousal maintenance.

Above all, keep this thought in mind…it will get better both financially and emotionally. Someday.

The instant replay:

1. Be Proactive

2. Don't have a pity party.
3. Be open and appropriate to other people in your children's lives.
4. Take control of finances

SUGGESTION #7

Never Use the Children as Foot Soldiers

If you could magnify the hurt you now feel from your divorce proceedings by one hundred, then maybe you can understand how your children feel. They have less knowledge and less control than you do. They are very vulnerable.

Do not assume because they are quiet that they are pain free. Their whole world is crumbling; they are scared and insecure and are depending entirely on their parents to help alleviate these fears.

So, don't do anything around your children to cause them any more pain.

1. Don't discuss the divorce in front of them.
2. Don't blame the other parent.
3. Don't discuss money problems.
4. Don't say derogatory things about the other parent. If you must vent, vent to an adult outside the earshot of the child.
5. Don't send messages back and forth to the other parent through your children. Communicate directly with the other parent, if not verbally, then by letter, email, or answering machine. I have found e-mail works well, because it's quick, short, and you can't shout over the computer. (Unless, like some people, you consider all capital letters to be shouting!)
6. Don't use kids in a power play. Power plays include bringing the kids home late, not being at home when visitation is supposed to start, threatening to cut visitation if other demands

are not met, not allowing the parent to see the kids if child support is not paid or not paid on time, etc. These "games" are not only immoral and wrong, they are most likely illegal. However, if there is a huge ongoing power play taking place it needs to be dealt with differently as discussed at the end of this chapter.

7. Don't interrogate the children about the other parent's home. However, do allow them to share their experiences of their "other" life. Do not use the information obtained by this sharing process against the other parent, ever, unless your child's safety is at stake. Likewise, do not tell them they can't tell the other parent anything about their life with you. Do not do anything in front of them that you wouldn't want the other parent to know, anyway (like fighting, screaming, dancing the Frug, etc.)
8. Do not interfere in your ex-spouse's household. Do not tell the children they don't have to obey the other parent's rules. Do not tell them they can come home if they are required to perform chores they do not wish to do. This is manipulative and devious behavior, but more importantly, it is detrimental to the children. You are not getting even with the other parent as much as you may think and you are definitely not buying your children's affections by allowing them to control and injure the other parent. What you are doing is damaging your children's ideas of fair play, integrity, respect for authority and self-esteem. You are damaging a very important relationship in their lives. Psychologists will tell you a positive relationship with both parents is essential to a healthy and responsible child. Why would you want to damage the most precious thing in your life?
9. If possible, be consistent with the other parent in discipline and rules for your children. Do not allow the children to play one side against the other. Teenagers are especially expert in this regard. (I sincerely think there must be secret courses teenagers take on "Bargaining and Blackmailing" to be able to get their own way in every conceivable circumstance.)

10. Do not try to get back at the other parent or play their game if they are trying to undermine your love, your home or your role. Stay a consistent and loving parent, and sooner or later your child will understand the inconsistencies that come from the "non-enlightened" parent and appreciate your approach much more. It may take months. It will probably take years. But stay the course and love them unconditionally and consistently. The stability that you project; the security that you provide; and, the love with which you surround them will pay off huge dividends. If they can have one household where they feel accepted, without conditions, they will normally gravitate there unconsciously.
11. Don't make excuses. (Here are just a few samples from the hundreds I've heard through the years.)
    a. "He's made my life miserable, so I'm going to make his a living hell"
    b. "He's a drunken sot, and I'll be damned if he ever sees the kids"
    c. "My in-laws are drunken sots, and I'll be damned if they ever see the kids."
    d. "My wife/husband is a bitch/bastard and I'll be damned is they ever see the kids."
    e. "I didn't want the divorce, so why should my kids or I have to suffer at all. He/she should just go away."
    f. "He/she is taking all the money and I have nothing left to buy those coveted salt and pepper shakers for the kids so I will make his/her life a living hell".

Get over it. You chose to marry this person and also made the decision to have children together. Make it as easy on your children as you possibly can. Do not put them in the middle.

Having said this, there are two exceptions of parental behavior that should not be overlooked. If these are present in your life, then you do have cause for concern and need more help than this little guidebook can give you.

First is Parental Alienation Syndrome (PAS), a condition when one parent completely turns the children against the other. I am sorry to say this is getting more and more prevalent and is usually achieved through continual manipulation and brainwashing of the children.

Parental Alienation Syndrome is not present just because the kids refuse to go to one parent. It is relatively normal when a child cries and becomes distressed at visitation transitions.

Parental Alienation Syndrome is often present when the children hate the other parent, want no contact whatsoever, and cannot go into detail as to why they have such intense feelings. The child will continually describe only one or two incidences, usually provided by their "chosen" parent and the reaction is out of proportion to the circumstances described. If you suspect PAS is affecting your relationship with the children, immediate and intensive help is needed. This is mind control manipulation on the part of the 'chosen' parent and is ongoing and intense. It is sick and completely destructive to the children involved.

The second parental behavior that must be addressed occurs where one parent has excessive power in the relationship. In any relationship one party usually has more control, but when this imbalance is so pronounced that it doesn't allow for normal interaction it becomes a problem.

Normally, this power imbalance is present during the marriage and divorce exacerbates the situation. This is manifested where one party feels as if he/she can do anything, and the rules do not apply to them. You will most likely see this problem at the very beginning of divorce proceedings, although sometimes it doesn't rear its ugly head until later.

Many times if one spouse has controlled the other during the relationship, but has been forced to give up this control because of the divorce, they will transfer this need to the parenting of the children and thus feel they still are able to control the spouse. This is a form of abuse and must be treated as such.

Any other form of abuse, whether it is physical, verbal or emotional also must be dealt with by a counselor, and all parameters of the visitation/custody schedule should be detailed by a professional or judge, with specific and immediate consequences if not adhered to.

Your attorney should be able to begin this counseling process through a court order. Mediation will not work in this instance. (Mediation is a process where both parties come together on an equal footing, in a neutral setting, and maturely discuss and solve problems with the help of a trained third party.) This process does not work where there is a power imbalance or abuse present.

Once a counselor is in place and has reviewed the situation, very specific guidelines must be set to control the time spent with the children. Although children should be interviewed and their concerns addressed, they must realize they are not in control and are not the responsible parties.

The counselor should set up detailed times and places for visitation, transportation and exchange orders, special events requirements (i.e., to minimize conflict, parents must sometimes divide the functions they are each able to attend; etc.) The counselor will also establish ways to avoid contact and conflict between the parents, and serious consequences if these orders are not adhered to.

Do not expect the abusive parent to comply. Remember, they think they are even above the court. What you are doing is documenting the disobedience (always have a witness with you at exchanges, events, etc.) and hopefully the court will soon tire of the constant disobedience of the non-conforming parent and inflict some sort of monetary or restrictive punishment to them. You and your attorney must be patient, strong and resolved to see this entire process through.

The review:

1. Don't do anything to hurt your children. Period!

SUGGESTION #8

Don't Get Remarried

Okay, remember how I have broken both Suggestions #1 and #2? Well, I have also broken this suggestion, which I'm sure really cements my credibility with you, dear reader. But who better than a guilty party, living through some very trying experiences I might add, is better equipped to give you insight into this potential nightmare.

If you have children, and you get remarried, you have now created what is termed a "blended family." You may think this name is derived from the word "blend" as defined in the dictionary: "To combine into an integrated whole, to produce a harmonious effect". Wrong. It really comes from the way one feels when placed inside a "blender" on chop mode for days at a time.

Take off those rose colored glasses and throw them away…now! Getting remarried with children in the equation is the hardest situation you will ever face. If the new spouse also has kids, the two sets of siblings will make World War Two look like a cakewalk. Conversely, if the new spouse has never had children, they will have absolutely no concept of what being a parent is all about, and therefore, they will think everything you do in the parenting role is not only wrong, but pathetic.

So, as neither option looks inviting…run! Run far, far away from another marriage. And as you will not take this advice anymore than you have my advice on marriage and divorce, let's see what we can do to improve the potential nightmare and upgrade it to only an uncomfortable dream.

First, and before the marriage even takes place, discuss how you will jointly handle money, space and rules in the home. These rules must be very minimal and basic such as no one can kill anyone. (This is literally the only rule I can think of that will most likely survive). Be consistent with both sub-families in the rules that you choose to enforce. Even more importantly, enforce them every time, with everyone.

Second, make sure there is a considerable amount of time for you to be with your children, independently from the other part of the "blended family". You don't all need to do everything together. You are not a Donna Reed family!

Third, and probably most important, take a refresher course in first aid.

Now comes the hard part. Only discipline your own children. Impossible, you say? What if they are acting up when their parent is not around? Who will stop them from destroying the house? How can I discipline my own child who is doing the same thing but not discipline my spouses' child. Well…I tried to tell you this blended family wouldn't work, didn't I?

Please notice that I said 'don't discipline your stepchildren,' I didn't say 'don't correct them.' Tell them what they are doing is inappropriate and hopefully this will alleviate the problem. Then, tell your spouse when convenient and assume they will take appropriate measures to discipline. But don't bet on it

Attempt to always be around your children during the initial blending of the family. Stories and blaming can get out of hand, and taking sides can cause a major rift between the newly formed unions. Example…wife tells hubby his child Tommy hit her child Chucky and she put Tommy in time out. Tommy tells dad that Chucky hit him first. Hubby tells wife Chucky hit first. Wife doesn't believe it. Hubby does and thinks the reprimand and discipline is wrong. Wife doesn't. Wife thinks hubby's kid is a brat. Hubby thinks wife's brat is a tattle tale…and those are the good days. It disintegrates from there.

Do not discipline the step kids, unless there is blood and video camera footage to back you up.

Do not criticize your stepchildren to their parent, a.k.a. your new spouse. It does no good, alienates you both, makes the other parent defensive and it usually backfires with them calling your children names. I have seen this rule broken numerous times and it usually ends with both parties tripping over each other to get to the phone to call their divorce attorneys.

Here is a suggestion of how to potentially influence the other parent to recognize the problem about which you are complaining (at least to some degree). If you do not criticize the stepchild, your spouse will not get defensive. If he is not defensive, he will therefore not feel the need to support his child, and will mumble under his breath when his kids do something inappropriate. He may actually handle the situation with correction or discipline, which is how it should be.

He will probably bring up his concerns at some future time if he doesn't feel as if you are criticizing his parenting. Most parents need to vent to an adult. Wait until he brings it up such as "Tommy can be such a little shit, why does he do those things?" You, through gritted teeth, then need to defend his kids at first, ("They're only little. Was it really that bad? It could have been worse…the cat's hair will grow back! The damage to the car was only $3700," etc.)

Once he/she does not feel you are attacking the children, they will usually allow their true responses to come out. At this point in time ask if there is anything you can do to help. Suggest some alternative consequences or reactions (still insisting that setting fire to the deck wasn't that bad).

The bottom line is that you have been given permission to add input into the situation without alienating your spouse. Your spouse has been given permission to vent without feeling obligated to defend his kids. This united front will also benefit the children through more consistent discipline.

It is critical that you both continue to discipline your own children in order to build a strong family relationship. On the other hand, if your spouse doesn't discipline to your liking and never vents about his children's behaviors, try to discuss specific examples without using superlatives…"Tommy always does"…or "Tommy never does." You might even try writing down specifics when they happen and save the discussion for a more non-threatening time. When appropriate, calmly ask what he thinks you both need to do when the kids act in certain ways and establish specific reactions and consequences. Remind him calmly the next time this behavior comes up and see if he follows the recourse you both discussed. If not, maybe it's time to visit a counselor.

Or, just skip all of the above and go straight to the counselor's office.

Just remember, you can say the most horrible things about people you love, but when someone else says the same exact thing about them you will go bananas. I call this the "banana theory." And when you put a banana in a blender, well you get the icky picture, so keep your opinions to yourself.

Now I am going to give you an amazing insight into this stepfamily fiasco. There is a reason that you can see your children clearly and know exactly what they need and why your spouse can't. (Here's a hint, they think exactly the same way about their kids.)

"How can my spouse be so hard on my kids, but not see how horrific his own children are," you lament. There is a reason and it is aptly referred to as the "emotional savings account principle." [1]

This principle explains just how your step kids can commit the most horrendous crimes against manners, common sense, and humanity and still be able to obtain unconditional love from their own parent.

The principle goes like this. When children are born, and for about the first 6-8 years, everyday you have enough love to give them and still put some back in a "love" savings account. This is because they are sweet and lovable…traits they will soon outgrow. Their love for you is overt and immense and that also is deposited into this account.

From about 8-11 years of age, there isn't a lot of excess love, so there aren't many deposits. But then again, there are few withdrawals.

But then comes those wonderful ages of 12 to14, where it would be more comfortable to pull your hair out than raise these charming angels! The stock market of love has just crashed and the "little shavers" start creating havoc. But not to worry, parents start withdrawing their "stored love" to compensate for this unique change of personality. Just a little at first, to get over the monthly mood swings and outbreak of pimples. But the withdrawals keep getting larger and more frequent. The children demand everything you have, they cannot see past the noses on their face, and they are so self-absorbed that they remind you of a sponge.

As the account dwindles, there is still the invested love in the parent's eyes and they continue to overlook the obvious serial killer they are raising. And then, just as emotional bankruptcy is looming in the distance, the child reaches eighteen and the aliens leave their bodies, just in the nick of time.

Remember, in all probability the stepparent does not have the luxury of this bank account of affection. They see the child in an objective, independent light...that is, if they are fair and mature. However, if they are insecure and feel they or their children are threatened, they will not only lose objectivity, but also be overly critical to compensate and feel powerful.

So, we as parents love and know our children better than anyone. I sincerely believe we know what is best for them and need to respect that quality in regard to our spouse. We never see our children as monsters, but as the sweet two-year-old sleeping with their teddy and giving us bear hugs for just being there. Remember, the stepparent feels this exact same way regarding their own children. Knowing this may help. Then again, it may not.

Recap:

1. Don't get remarried.
2. Don't marry someone unless both sets of children are perfect and need no discipline whatsoever.
3. Don't criticize the "little shavers," even if they shave the cat.
4. Don't worry, someday they will all grow up and leave the house...if you're lucky.

[1] The Emotional Bank Account, proffered by Stephen R. Covey in his highly acclaimed *The Seven Habits of Highly Effective People*, is a "metaphor for the amount of trust in a relationship." With all due respect to Mr. Covey, I have taken the liberty of also adopting these wonderful words to the love all parents feel for their children, and the emotional "deposits" and corresponding "withdrawals" they make to and from us as they mature.

SUGGESTION #9

Don't Forget to Discover Something Bigger than Yourself

During a divorce, emotions are so intense and ever present that the degree of time, energy and attention necessary to just maneuver day-to-day activities is overwhelming. You now have complete responsibility for the kids, the home, the income, the laundry, and the cat. Your heart is breaking, or you are in a new and unnerving environment, or you feel guilty, or you just feel numb. You are overcome with your problems and cannot imagine life will ever get back to normal. You are depressed, obsessed, repressed. No matter how much you try, you never have enough money, or time, or sleep. A walking zombie has more personality than you. I have been there, done that. I empathize.

Although you are completely drained and out of control, now is the time to stop, take a deep breath, get down on your knees and ask a Higher Power for help. You can't do it by yourself anymore. You actually never could, but the pretense was available. It is not available now. Let down your pride and your prejudice. Lift your concerns up to a Higher Being. Sometimes your troubles are so immense you can't even verbalize what they are. Its okay, He can. Just start talking to Him.

You need to discover something Bigger than yourself, as self is the only thing that you have been able to think about lately, and rightly so. I remember getting sick of myself and my problems during my divorce, and not being able to get away from me, no matter how hard I tried.

I needed a different perspective, a different way of looking at things, to see a *bigger picture*, to be able to count my blessings. And through

Him, I discovered I still had so many. I discovered things could be much worse. I discovered I needed a peace that no attorney or court or counselor or spouse could give me.

St. Augustine remarked some fifteen hundred years ago, "Our hearts will never be at rest away from the One who made them." It is still true today, especially in times of distress.

I tried to quit thinking about myself in just those terms...myself...and tried to start appreciating other things, other people, other activities. I realized self-pity was unproductive as well as unattractive. I realized I needed more than pity; I needed a very large "Shoulder" to cry on. But more than that, Someone to help me get over the crying and on with the living. It didn't come all at once. It came in waves and in degrees. But it did come. And He will come to you if you just ask.

But don't forget to quiet your soul and also listen.

You may have always been spiritual. Take this time to renew and reconnect. You may have never been spiritual. Take this time to explore the spiritual mysteries.

You may not want to become spiritual, and although I feel that's like saying "I don't want to breathe clean air or be happy," that's your right. I would sincerely suggest that you still try to find something bigger than your problems and become immersed in it. Volunteer at a homeless shelter, tutor a child, collect signatures for an environmental cause, or seek donations for a favorite charity. The point is to do something for someone else who has a real need. It will literally help fulfill whatever need you may have.

This Bigger Being is the only place you can turn to give you the peace and the energy needed to live your life day-to-day, year-to-year. It's yours for the asking. All you need to do is ask.

Mother Teresa said, "Ask and seek and your heart will grow big enough to receive Him and to keep Him as your own. Wherever God has put you, that is your vocation. It is not what we do, but how much love we put into it."

Got God?

Review:

1. Get God.

SUGGESTION #10

Don't Forget to Live Happily Ever After

Your life is not ruined. Someday it will be better than ever. Cherish the time you have with your children and family and don't dwell on the negatives. The truly successful life is not measured at the end of the life. It is measured at the end of each day. If you have more happy moments than sad ones, that day was a success.

Practice this ritual. At the end of each day as you lie in bed, clear your mind and for five minutes remember the happy moments of the day; a blue sky, your child's voice or smile, a joke, a soothing song, a pretty picture. Five minutes is a long time to think of "moments." Soon, all day long you will be looking for some happy moments to "remember," or to make. You'll spend your whole day looking for happy times, and the times will become happier.

I know it's hard to be happy if you didn't want this divorce, or if you have financial troubles, or you don't have as much time with your children as you desire. There is no winning in a divorce. It's a passage in life.

Appreciate the time you do have and make today a success. The journey is its own reward. Ask for help along the way if you get lost. (Men have an especially hard time with this one.) Know there is light at the end of the tunnel.

"Even in the mundane, the extraordinary exists. We can make sacred everything we do by attentiveness and compassion. We must recommit ourselves daily. It requires regular exercise." *If not now, When?* Stephanie Marston.

You have been given a great gift…a new day, a chance to choose. "Nothing splendid has been achieved except by those who dared to believe that something inside them was superior to circumstances." Bruce Barton.

My favorite morning devotion is the following from the book, *With My Whole Heart*, by Karen Burton Mains:

> "Most of us have forgotten how to greet the day. The knowledge is all but lost to us that a new day is sacred, a gift from God, a rare and precious gift. A new day brings with it another opportunity to start all over, to raise one's head from the pillow with a glad heart, to watch the clouds roll across the dark sky now diffusing pink, and to breathe that child prayer of gratitude 'Oh God, life again. Again, one more day of life.'
>
> We must relearn how to stand in awe, how to face for a moment the eastern sky with praise and thanksgiving and allow our hearts to be filled with a corresponding inner daybreak of adoration.
>
> We must learn to not ever take for granted—no matter how pain-filled our life—that we are alive and the earth still turns on its axis, that evil has not wobbled the world off its course while we slept and we must understand this sacramental symbol, this reenactment of life which comes resurrecting every twenty-four hours.
>
> Celebrating each new day helps us develop the ability to be grateful for all new moments and for the God who is in each one. The discipline of celebrating each new day influences our attitude toward all of life.
>
> A new day signifies The Lord of morning is still sovereign over the world."

Treat your ex-spouse with integrity and you then have a right to hold your head high. You cannot help how you are being treated, only how you choose to treat people, situations and life. As long as you are true to yourself, your values and ideals, you will live happily ever after.

"Everything can be taken from a person but…the last of the human freedoms—to choose one's attitude in any given set of circumstances, to choose one's own way." *Man's Search for Meaning.* Victor E. Frankl

Take chances. "Life is a crapshoot." Anonymous

"And the trouble is, if you don't risk anything, you risk even more." Erica Jong.

You are strong. You have survived. You are smart. My wish is that you will take advantage of the great adventures your new life will reveal…that you will decide today to take chances…and that you will grow and be happy.

"And the day came when the risk to remain in the bud was more painful than the risk it took to bloom." Anais Nin.

Review:
Live Happily…Today…and Ever After.